FRIGHTENING FLEAS

by Meish Goldish

Consultant: Paula L. Marcet, PhD
Research Biologist
Atlanta, Georgia

BEARPORT
PUBLISHING

New York, New York

Credits

Cover, © Jiri Prochazka/Shutterstock and © Cosmin Manci/Shutterstock; TOC, © Cosmin Manci/Shutterstock; 4, © Ting-Li Wang/The New York Times/Redux Pictures; 5, © F1online digitale Bildagentur GmbH/Alamy; 6L, © James Cavallini/BSIP/Newscom; 6R, © Gado Images/Alamy; 7, © Rick Scibelli/The New York Times/Redux Pictures; 8T, © Scooperdigital/iStock; 8B, © Paulo Oliveira/Alamy; 9, © Photo 12/Alamy; 10, © Paulo Oliveira/Alamy; 11L, © Comel Constantin/Shutterstock; 11R, © Cultura Creative/Alamy; 12L, © Rod Lamkey Jr.; 12R, © BonNontawat/Shutterstock; 13T, © erniedecker/iStock; 13B, © Science History Images/Alamy; 14, © chendongshan/iStock; 15L, © Manuel-F-O/iStock; 15R, © anamariategzes/iStock; 16, © blickwinkel/Alamy; 17, © Creative Mood/Shutterstock; 18, © coopder1/iStock; 19T, © E_serebryakova/Shutterstock; 19B, © Coco Rattanakorn/Shutterstock; 20, © Pavel Krasensky/Shutterstock; 21T, © Pavel Rodimov/Dreamstime; 21B, © tdub303/iStock; 22 (T to B), © Juan Gaertner/Shutterstock, © Kateryna Kon/Shutterstock, and © The Natural History Museum/Alamy.

Publisher: Kenn Goin
Senior Editor: Joyce Tavolacci
Creative Director: Spencer Brinker
Photo Researcher: Thomas Persano

Library of Congress Cataloging-in-Publication Data

Names: Goldish, Meish, author.
Title: Frightening fleas / by Meish Goldish.
Description: New York, New York : Bearport Publishing, [2019] | Series:
    Bugged out! the world's most dangerous bugs |
    Includes bibliographical references and index.
Identifiers: LCCN 2018047053 (print) | LCCN 2018048348 (ebook) | ISBN
    9781642802382 (ebook) | ISBN 9781642801699 (library)
Subjects: LCSH: Fleas as carriers of disease—Juvenile literature. |
    Fleas—Juvenile literature.
Classification: LCC RA641.F5 (ebook) | LCC RA641.F5 G65 2019 (print) | DDC
    614.4/324—dc23
LC record available at https://lccn.loc.gov/2018047053

For more information, write to Bearport Publishing Company, Inc., 45 West 21st Street, Suite 3B, New York, New York 10010. Printed in the United States of America.

10 9 8 7 6 5 4 3 2 1

Contents

The Plague!

In November 2002, John Tull and his wife, Lucinda Marker, were visiting New York City when they both fell deathly ill. They had pounding headaches, strange swellings, and bone-crushing body aches. "It felt like our skin hurt," Lucinda said. At the hospital, doctors were puzzled. What was making the couple so seriously sick?

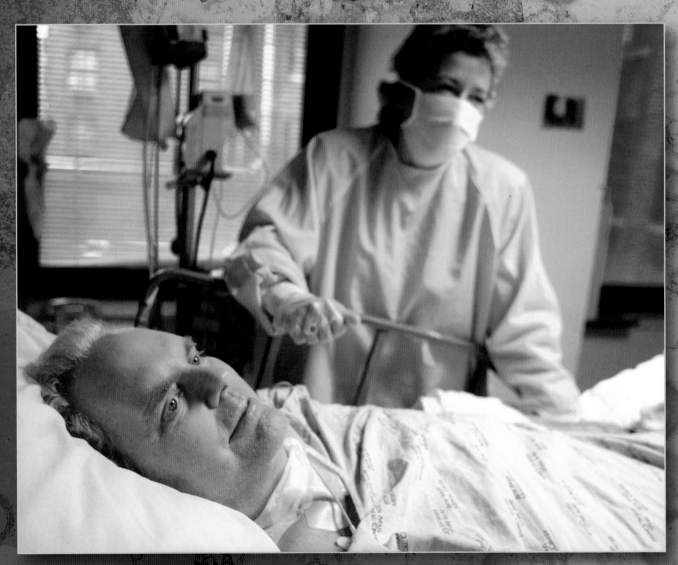

John Tull rests in a hospital bed with Lucinda at his side.

Doctors then made a startling discovery. Blood tests revealed that John and Lucinda had bubonic plague. The plague is a **rare** and deadly disease transmitted by fleas. It was the first case in New York City in over 100 years! To treat the illness, doctors gave the couple **antibiotics**. Lucinda recovered in just a few days. However, John remained very ill. His fingers and toes turned black as the **infection** spread. Would he survive the plague?

The plague is most often spread to people through a bite from an infected flea. John and Lucinda were probably bitten by fleas near their home in New Mexico before coming to New York.

A flea is a tiny, wingless insect with strong legs that can spread disease to people and other animals.

A Long Battle

John lay near death in the hospital. To keep his body from breaking down further, doctors placed him in a **coma**. Special machines helped him breathe. Doctors then made a **drastic** decision to save John's life. They cut off both his legs below the knees to stop the deadly infection from spreading throughout his body!

Buboes

A close-up view of the tiny life-forms, called *Yersinia pestis*, that cause the plague.

Many people who have the plague develop painful, dark-colored swellings called buboes (BOO-bohs). These buboes are what gave the bubonic plague its name.

Slowly, John began to recover. Amazingly, after 224 days in the hospital, he was well enough to go home. However, John still faced many challenges. He had to learn to walk with new **prosthetic** legs. "It was like he was a baby, learning how to do everything again," Lucinda said. With her help, John succeeded. "We became a team at living life," she said.

With Lucinda by his side, John learned how to walk with his new legs.
Sadly, in 2014, he died from a medical condition unrelated to the plague.

Spreading Disease

How does a tiny flea spread bubonic plague? Fleas feed on the blood of animals, including humans. When a flea bites an animal that has the plague, the insect sucks plague **bacteria** into its body. It then becomes a carrier of the disease.

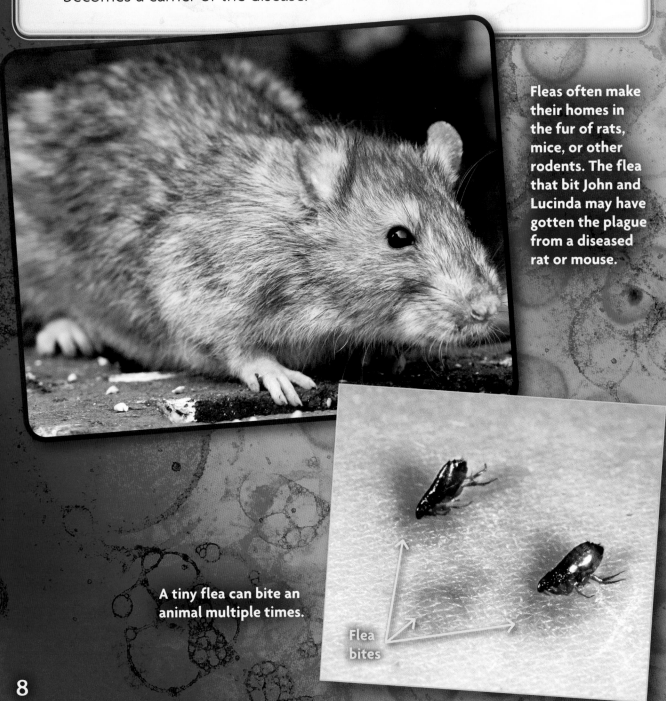

Fleas often make their homes in the fur of rats, mice, or other rodents. The flea that bit John and Lucinda may have gotten the plague from a diseased rat or mouse.

A tiny flea can bite an animal multiple times.

Flea bites

Later, the bacteria-carrying flea may bite a human. Plague bacteria from the insect enter the person through the tiny bite holes. Once the bacteria make their way into the person's bloodstream, the bite victim gets the plague and becomes very sick—just as John and Lucinda did.

An Italian painting from 1349 that shows plague victims being buried

Between 1346 and 1353, more than 20 million people in Europe died of bubonic plague, also known then as the Black Death. It's believed that fleas got the plague from rats and then passed it on to humans.

Built to Bite

Because it can **transmit** diseases, a flea can be deadly—despite its tiny size. A flea is only about 0.06 to 0.8 inches (1.5 to 20 mm) long. That's a little larger than the period at the end of this sentence. Yet the teeny insect is a powerful biting machine.

A close-up view of a flea jumping into the air

To reach its **prey**, a flea can jump up to 8 inches (20 cm)—that's about 150 times its own height. If a person could do that, he or she would be able to leap over buildings eight stories tall!

A flea's body is narrow with flat sides. Its shape allows it to easily move through a victim's hair or fur to reach skin. Each of a flea's six strong legs has claws at the end. They help the insect to hold on tight to its prey. When it's ready to bite, a flea slices into an animal's flesh with its sharp **mandibles**. Finally, it inserts a straw-like **proboscis** to suck its victim's blood.

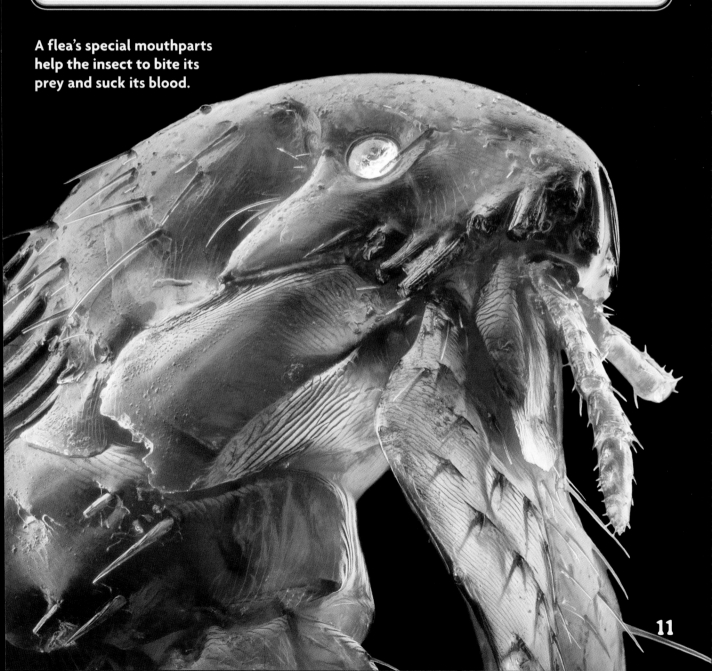

A flea's special mouthparts help the insect to bite its prey and suck its blood.

Terrible Typhus

Bubonic plague isn't the only deadly disease that fleas can transmit. Sarah Strickland, a student in Texas, learned this firsthand. In 2009, she suddenly developed a throbbing headache, chills, high fever, and a rash on her **abdomen**. At first, doctors thought her illness was a virus that would go away on its own. "They said it would clear up, that I'd be fine," said Sarah. They were wrong.

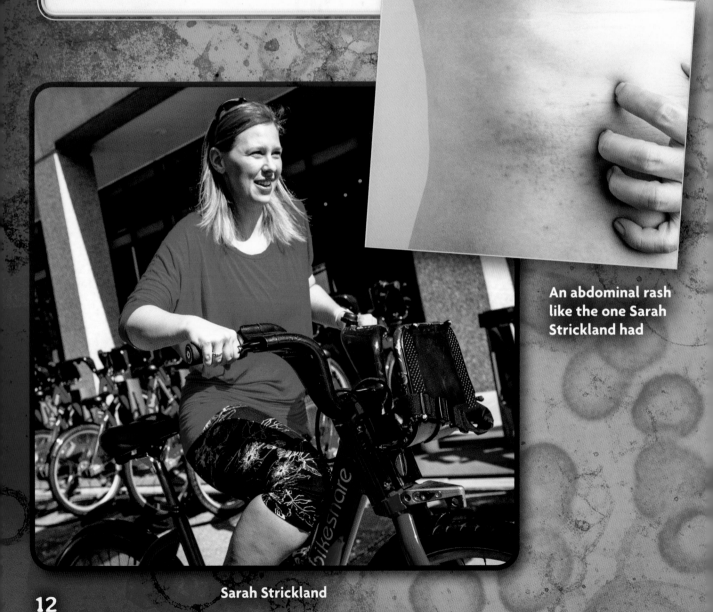

An abdominal rash like the one Sarah Strickland had

Sarah Strickland

Sarah grew sicker by the day. Finally, blood tests showed that she had a dangerous disease called typhus. Before Sarah became ill, opossums had nested inside the walls of her home. The unwanted furry guests had fleas that carried the bacteria that cause typhus. After being bitten by one of the fleas, Sarah likely scratched the wound, infecting herself with bacteria-filled flea poop. After her **diagnosis**, doctors gave Sarah antibiotics and she began to recover. However, it took a full year for her to regain her strength.

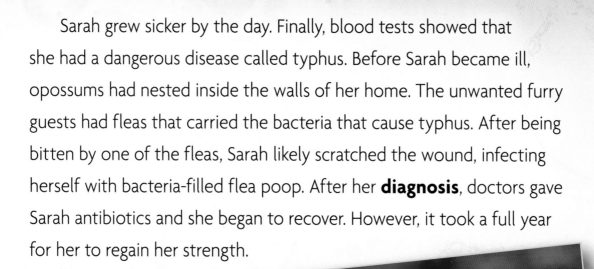

An opossum

After Sarah's illness, Kristy Murray, a scientist, noticed many more cases of typhus occurring in Texas. "People need to put typhus on their **radar**," she said. "This is a big comeback."

A close-up view of the bacteria *Rickettsia typhi* that cause typhus

At Home on a Body

Fleas make their homes all over the world. They are known as **external parasites** because they live on animals or people in order to suck their blood. However, not all kinds carry deadly diseases. In North America, there are about 250 different kinds of fleas, but only about 30 kinds transmit diseases. One of the most common disease carriers is the cat flea. It can transmit typhus and bartonellosis, among other illnesses.

A cat scratches fleabites.

The cat flea most often lives in the fur of cats and dogs. In addition to diseases, the flea's **host** can suffer uncomfortable itching and **irritated** skin. Other kinds of fleas live on other warm-blooded animals, including squirrels, rats, rabbits, and occasionally birds.

This dog is biting its irritated leg after being bitten by cat fleas.

Fleas sometimes rest on clothes, blankets, or an item close to a person's skin. When they want to feed, the fleas leap from the item to the person.

This person's leg was badly bitten by fleas, causing many red marks on the skin.

A Flea's Life

There are trillions of fleas around the world. One reason for this is that fleas reproduce very quickly. One female flea can lay more than 5,000 eggs in her lifetime! Depending on the type of flea, she may lay up to 30 eggs at a time. The eggs take around two weeks to hatch.

A water flea carries her eggs inside her body.

Eggs

With enough blood to eat, a flea can live about two to three months. However, some fleas may live up to a year and a half!

A flea **larva** hatches out of each egg. The wormlike larva stays in a dark place, such as under a carpet or blanket, and feeds. The larva eats dead insects and flea **feces**. Soon, it weaves a **cocoon** and becomes a **pupa**. After about four days, the pupa turns into a bloodthirsty adult.

FLEA
LIFE CYCLE

ADULT FLEA

FLEA EGGS

FLEA LARVA

FLEA PUPA

This chart shows the stages of a cat flea's life.

Lost Sight

Often, people become ill after being bitten by bacteria-carrying fleas. However, fleas can also sicken people without ever touching them. One morning in 2015, Janese Walters of Toledo, Ohio, woke up blind in one eye. Doctors couldn't figure out why—even after months of medical testing.

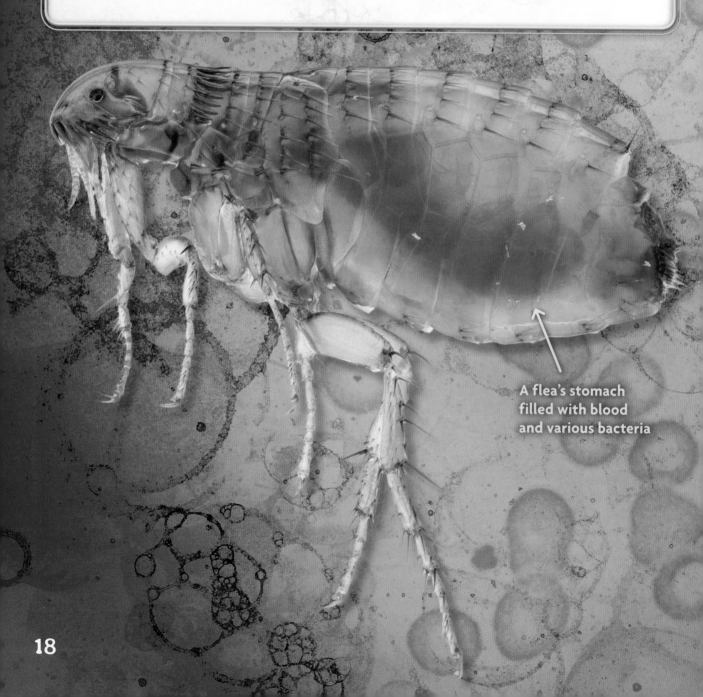

A flea's stomach filled with blood and various bacteria

Finally, Janese mentioned that she had a pet cat. Doctors figured out that the cat was a carrier of a flea-**borne** disease called cat scratch fever. At some point, the cat probably licked Janese's eye. Then she got cat scratch fever, which caused her blindness. Doctors don't think her lost sight will ever return. Yet Janese is still grateful. "I'm just lucky it didn't spread to my other eye," she said.

Cat owners should be careful to avoid getting scratched, bitten, or licked by their pet. Also, they should always wash their hands after playing with their cat and clean any scratches or cuts.

People can get cat scratch fever from the bite or scratch of an infected cat. They can also get the disease if **saliva** from an infected cat gets into an open **wound** or touches the white part of a person's eye.

A Serious Problem

In recent years, the number of people who have gotten ill from fleabites has risen sharply. Scientists think the increase may be due to **climate change**. Fleas are increasing in numbers and spreading to new places because of the warmer weather. As a result, more people are being bitten by infected fleas. Lyle Petersen, an expert in insect diseases, warns, "This is a long-term problem that requires action."

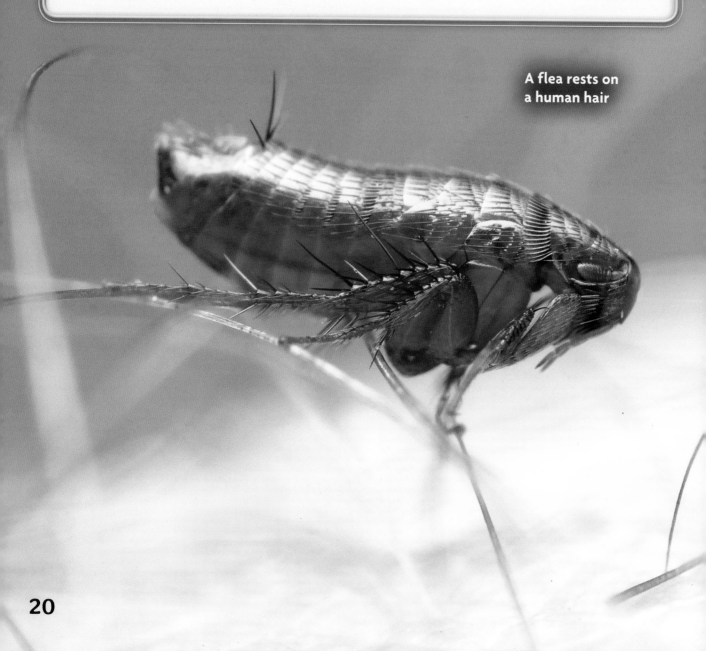

A flea rests on a human hair

What can people do to protect themselves? Pet owners should bathe their animals regularly and put flea collars on them. Pets can also be given special medicines and other products that control fleas. Vacuuming carpets and rugs at home is also important. All of these steps can help both pets and people stay safe from dangerous flea-borne diseases.

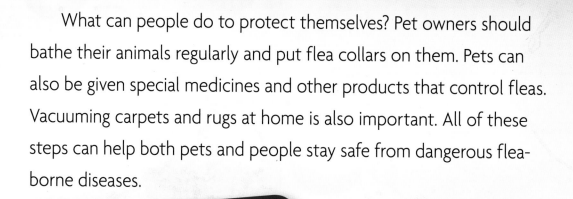

Flea-control drops and shampoos help keep fleas off dogs.

People bitten by a flea should wash the bite with soap and water. They should not scratch the bite, which can spread the infection. If their condition worsens, bite victims should see a doctor.

Other Flea-Borne Diseases

In addition to bubonic plague, typhus, and cat scratch fever, infected fleas can transmit a number of other diseases. Here are some of them:

Tapeworm

A tapeworm is a parasite that lives in the guts of dogs, cats, and humans. It has a long, ribbon-like body and a small head with hooked teeth. These worms must complete their life cycle within flea larvae. Children or pets can get tapeworms by swallowing infected fleas.

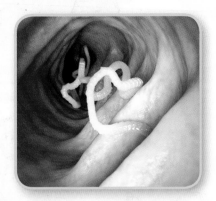

An image of a tapeworm in human intestines

Tularemia

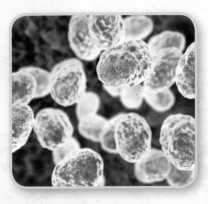

Tularemia bacteria

Tularemia, also called rabbit fever, is a disease caused by bacteria that's often transmitted by fleas or other insects. The fleas typically live on diseased rabbits and rats. In humans, tularemia causes fever, skin sores, body pain, weakness, and, sometimes, death.

Tungiasis

This disease occurs when the tiny tunga flea, which is native to islands in the Caribbean Sea, **burrows** into a person's skin to feed on blood. Often, the disease causes sores on the skin and can lead to infections. Tungiasis sometimes heals on its own after a person's skin cells shed and the flea dies, but it usually requires treatment.

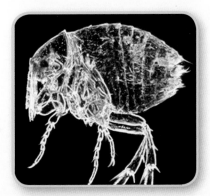

A tunga, or chigoe, flea

Glossary

abdomen (AB-duh-muhn) the belly, or middle part, of a human's or an insect's body

antibiotics (an-ti-bye-OT-iks) medicines used to destroy or stop the growth of bacteria that cause diseases

bacteria (bac-TIHR-ee-uh) tiny life-forms that can cause disease

borne (BORN) carried or transported by

burrows (BUR-ohz) digs into something solid

climate change (KLYE-mit CHAYNJ) the warming of Earth due to environmental changes, such as a buildup of greenhouse gases that trap the sun's heat

cocoon (kuh-KOON) a covering that some insects make from silky threads as they develop into adults

coma (KOH-muh) a state of deep unconsciousness caused by an injury, illness, or drugs

diagnosis (dye-uhg-NOH-sis) the identification of a disease or illness

drastic (DRASS-tik) sudden or extreme action

external parasites (ek-STUR-nuhl PA-ruh-sites) organisms that get food by living on other organisms

feces (FEE-seez) solid body waste

host (HOHST) an animal or plant from which a parasite gets nutrition

infection (in-FEK-shuhn) an illness caused by germs entering the body

irritated (ihr-uh-TAY-tid) becoming painful or red

larva (LAR-vuh) a young insect

mandibles (MAN-duh-buhlz) biting or sucking mouthparts

prey (PRAY) an animal that is hunted and eaten by another animal

proboscis (pruh-BOS-uhss) the long, tube-like nose or mouthpart of some insects that's used for feeding

prosthetic (pross-THET-ik) an artificial device that replaces a missing body part

pupa (PYOO-puh) the stage of development in which an insect changes from a larva to an adult

radar (RAY-dar) range of notice or awareness

rare (RAIR) not often found or seen

saliva (suh-LYE-vah) a clear liquid produced in the mouths of many animals that helps them eat and break down food

transmit (tranz-MIT) pass something from one being to another

wound (WOOND) an injury in which a person's body is cut and damaged

Index

Bibliography

Mehlhorn, Heinz. *Animal Parasites: Diagnosis, Treatment, Prevention.* Düsseldorf, Germany: Springer (2016).

Twist, Clint. *The Life Cycle of Fleas (Creepy Crawlies).* Mankato, MN: New Forest Press (2013).

Read More

Keiser, Cody. *Fleas (Freaky Freeloaders: Bugs That Feed on People).* New York: PowerKids Press (2015).

Somervill, Barbara A. *Fleas: Feasting on Blood (Bloodsuckers).* New York: PowerKids Press (2008).

Learn More Online

To learn more about fleas, visit
www.bearportpublishing.com/BuggedOut

About the Author

Meish Goldish has written more than 300 books for children. He lives in Brooklyn, New York.